This book is a gift

From

To

Date

LETTER TO MY FATHER

JOY DANIEL

Letter To My Father

ISBN:

December, 2022

DEDICATION

This book is dedicated to God, the giver of life and the lives that have returned to be with him. May the soul of my Father, and others keep resting in peace.

ACKNOWLEDGEMENT

My ultimate gratitude goes to God who makes all this possible and beautiful in their time. My appreciation goes to the Daniel's and Ebo's, friends (Ibukunoluwa, Deyinka, Pato and Uloma) and mentors (Mr Lateef Kelani, Dr. Segun Jegede) for their support morally and financially.

Also, I am grateful to my editor, Adepoju Samuel, for his guidance while writing this piece. I also want to appreciate my lecturers in the Department of English, especially those who supported and encouraged me to keep writing projects at the company. Thanks to them, I not only improved as a writer but also as a leader in the writing department.

With you all standing behind me, I am confident in the path I'm toeing. It is my prayer that you'd find people lined up at your back whenever you need them.

Kneading Hope

...though through tears ad pain, my lips still part in smiles

The journey is an everest-labour, hence I have some tears

But why cry, when it can be made an array of false-faced textiles?

So I guard my loins as I face my fears.

I miss your presence, and I still wish I can turn the tide

True and through, under the confluence of hope I hide:

We will meet again, and rejoice to see

Your hard-borne voyage, a virile warrior it made me.

Dear Dad,

I don't want to do this for I am confident no replies would come from you; but still, I write because I need someone to rant to, someone to listen without any interruption. Clearly, you fit that description, so, here I am. Since I am your precious daughter, you may know how I feel. After all, you'll understand me even if I don't make any sense to others.

How are you doing, dad? Should I even be asking that when I know that I'd definitely never get an answer to it? You are presumably doing better than we are and need no one to fuss about you. Yet I can't help but think if you are doing well wherever you may be. Hey, dad, I think that you are doing just great because mama said so.

How many years has it been again? Did you lose a tally of it? Well, you may since you are not the one at the receiving end of your departure. Life's not been the same with your wife and children because we keep track of the years ever since you left. It's even worse for me because of the particular month you disappeared. Why you had to go in that very month remains a mystery to me. Worse still, it is something I may spend the rest of my existence brooding over without finding a logical answer; this I fear might leave me very miserable till I'm able to see you again.

It's been 17 years of continuous pungent tears cascading down our hopelessly hopeful faces, 17 horrible years of the seemingly hard life that your absence exposed us to, 17 years of *unprotectedness*, and 17 years of having to deal with your indifferent and highly greedy family. 17 solid years, dad, have rolled by. Do you even know this?

Do you occasionally think about what sort of men leave their thirty-two years old wife and four poor children behind for so long? Or do you just naturally carry on with your other life like nothing ever happened? I wish I had written to you earlier than now. Perhaps, I might just be reading your replies to my endless questions if it were possible for you to write back. Believe me, dad, that I had to gather this unnecessary courage to write to you after so many years which I had wanted to do on several occasions. Still, I couldn't bring myself to do it as it seems that I am the most broken by your absence and need the most healing processes to come to terms with the frigid reality that has always been viciously staring at me for the past years.

How do I undo the haunting memory of you departing just a few days before my fifth birthday? It is still excruciating. It was on the 13th of January, 2005. I could still faintly reminisce about the gathering of some people in front of our home very early in the morning. Although mom thinks that I was too young to have such memories of the distant past, I do. Really, dad, I remember that day: one old aunt had come to take me and little Willie, who was just two months old, to her place that morning; something that had never occurred before. She was extremely nice to us that day and I remember how she kept saying, "Suzanne is going to have a hard time looking at your face every day. You look exactly like your father." I wondered why my face would be a problem for her since she had always shown extra love to me because I have your face. I couldn't wait for mom to come to get us that day. I just wanted to get away from the old lady's not-very-tidy cottage which reeked of animal dung as she reared some animals in the backyard of her little house. Her friendly attribute was a stark contrast to her house. I remember that I didn't get to eat breakfast with you that morning, and neither did we have dinner together because I and little Willie ended up sleeping in that cottage. Little Willie kept waking up in the night intermittently because he needed to suckle, his hungry cries woke me up quicker than they did the old lady whose snores reverberated in her tiny room. The little time I closed my eyes to sleep, I nearly got choked up by the offending foul whiff that followed the old lady's loud farts. Sincerely, I fervently prayed the night away and prevailed on the old lady to take us home. Unfortunately for us, mom didn't come for us, instead the old lady took Willie to mom to suckle and brought him back. After about nine days, mom came to the cottage accompanied by two other women to get us. Ahhh, dad, you should have seen how I let out a deep sigh of relief having escaped the hazardous exhalation and isolation in that cottage.

To say that I was disappointed and I still am on getting home and meeting with your sudden absence was and it's still an understatement. Also, something, I subtly noticed, was off about mom's appearance. Her head was shaved and she was clothed in a black gown. she had her head wrapped with a black scarf, her lips were dry and, her voice cracked with her whole pale appearance.

“Mom, ” I beckoned to your wife, “where is dad?” I asked after she had turned to face me. She just stood there transfixed and it looked like she was never going to give an answer to my question. She walked over to the long chair where we normally sat to eat and looked me in the face intently. That was the first time she had looked at me that way. Instantly I could sense in my innocent little mind that what would come of her buccal wasn't going to be something mild. “Angela, you see, he left yesterday….”

“Is that why you didn’t come to get us since?”

“Yes, I had to stay with him for three days before he left...”

“Mom, where did he go?, he didn’t say he was going anywhere, ” I cut in.

“He didn’t say where he left for and since you might ask when he’ll be back, he might probably never come back. So we have to live well until we can meet him where he went to, do you understand me?” she asked sorrowfully while pestered her with more questions. It was glaring that she wasn’t in the mood to answer my many questions about the man who just deserted her, so I stopped probing.

So, it painfully happened that nobody remembered my seventh birthday as the air in the house was chilly cold, reeking of the stench of a departed figure. I don't quite recall if anyone even wished me a happy birthday because someone chose to leave a few days before the day I was born. Sadly, it has been that way up until now. I haven't celebrated any birthday since I was born or maybe since I could remember. Back then, I think the constant troubling thoughts on how to raise three girls and a boy all by herself blocked mom's recollection of important dates. I still think that Tope calls to remind her to call me on my birthdays these past few years; it just stings. Anyways, I won't hold it against her because you paved the way for all these occurrences so much that the banks wished me even before I could say a prayer for myself for I always had to start preparing myself mentally days before my birthday every year. For me and undoubtedly for mom, it's a remembrance of absence rather than a celebration of my life. With all truthfulness, this makes me jealous that even in your absence, people can't still see me for me, rather they see me for you. How long I have to put up with this, I do not know.

Dad, I've started the usual ritual before my birthday this year. However, it's going to be a lot different from what has been happening over the years. I'm going to celebrate my silver jubilee in two days ahead, and I want to be able to move away from under your shadows and live my own life, being happy whenever I can. I won't be writing about how much I miss you and I want you to come back, and neither will I be crying on my birthday that my best friend and dad aren't around to wish me and make the iconic eggs soup for me. No, I won't be doing all that moping. I'm going to throw a party and celebrate with your wife, other children, the children in the neighbourhood orphanage, and my friends. You are not going to be too angry about this, are you? It may upset mom a little but even she has been encouraging me to be happy as much as possible. Hence, I speculate that she won't be disappointed with my actions.

Dad, isn't it great that I decided to write to you to intimate you about the life you have missed out on? Don't worry I won't be too wordy because I know that you are or were a man of few words. Although I am sure, you never got bored with mom's endless philippic. But, believe me to make it brief as it seems that I inherited almost all your traits. I am not looking forward to seeing any reply to my missives as I'm too understanding to know that it might not be convenient for you since you weren't even expecting to see my letter after so long a duration.

Dad, don't be overly disappointed at my inability to vividly recall all that happened, you shouldn't really, I was only seven years of age and mom praises me a lot for having such a sharp memory, unlike others. I remembered that after some time in Akeh, mom decided that it was time to go back home. Unfortunately, she had a disagreement with your family over the custody of her own children. I guess she won thankfully because we all followed her wherever she went.

We visited her oldest sister, Aunty Mani who lived in a nearby town. I can not describe her attitude towards us but I'm sure she warmly received us as mom is always grateful to her whenever she remembers those times we spent in her house. We must have stayed for close to a year or more than that as I was able to speak a bit of my uncle's language. Our next stop was at Uncle Ben's home, mom's immediate older brother who was married to one of the most impish women that ever walked this planet. Uncle Ben was obviously very happy to see his younger sister and us. Oh! I forgot that I didn't mention that mom sent Tope and Lilian ahead to somewhere I didn't know. In fact, I had almost forgotten that I had two older sisters during our nomadic years. Aunty Ope, my uncle's wife, told mom to move into the smaller quarters at the back of the house while uncle was not around one day; it was just about four days after our arrival. She gave mom a small mattress that could barely contain two slim bodies, a stove, and two small pots. The quarter looked tiny but had a bathroom in it. Mom broke down in hysterical wailing, the like I had never seen her do before and she kept yelling at God, "What is my sin oh Lord, why is this happening to me? Why?" I wondered back then if God ever answered her many questions. She stopped abruptly when she realized that I was weeping along with her.

"Joy, stop crying my child, mom was just tired that's why mom was crying," she consoled me and gave me a very tight embrace.

Uncle Ben got back from work that day looking for us his wife was not around. He came to the backyard to search for us as he couldn't find us in the main house.

"Suzzane, I've been looking all over the house for you people. Why are you here?" he asked as he picked up little Willie in his hands and played with him.

"Ah, brother, I asked Ope if we could stay here. You know how big Williams is, he walks everywhere and might start breaking things in the house if he wanders too much. We are ok here" mom explained to cover up for her wife's actions.

"This place will be too cold for the children at night and this bed is too small for the three of you. You should come back into the main building please, there are enough rooms there," he persuaded mom.

"Let us stay here tonight, if I find it too cold for them, I will come back," mom replied.

"Ok, then, I'll see you later," he said, as he put sleepy Williams on the bed, he ruffled my hair and smiled brightly at me before he exited the room.

Aunty Ope brought our dinner that evening. Mom was so thankful to her because she knew we, her children, were on the verge of bursting into cries and causing her headache due to starvation. We indeed caused a frenzy with our loud sobs as the first spoon of the rice and stew was like a volcanic eruption on our taste buds. On realising how peppery the food was, mom packed the stew atop the white rice and made us eat white rice without stew, she kept fighting back the huge balls of tears formed in her beautiful eyes, the ones she couldn't control that dashed down her pale and dry cheeks were wiped with the edge of her wrapper as she kept encouraging me to eat more. That night, mom laid me on the mattress beside her after she had prayed and cried intermittently in between her prayers. She slept facing up and laid Williams on her chest: that was how we slept.

Very early the following dawn, we were awoken suddenly from sleep by the loud noise echoing in the compound, the noise got louder, as Uncle knocked and asked mom to step out into the compound. Mom strapped Williams on her back and stepped out hurriedly, I followed behind her.

"Suzzane, why did you lie to me about your movement into the boys' quarters?" Uncle Ben thundered with so much anger. Mom didn't answer. It was glaring that her brother had found out from his wife that she orchestrated our movement into the quarters. Mom looked at Aunty Ope who was steaming with resentment. She also had a baby girl of Williams' age strapped to her back.

"Brother…." Mom started but was cut short by her brother. "I know everything that happened, so don't just open your mouth to utter more lies. Just make sure you move back into the main house before I come from work today, do you hear me?" he asked and stormed out of the compound giving his wife a hard glare, the wife re-directed the favour by staring mischievously at us and topped it with an iconic hiss as she walked passed us.

We didn't move into the main house that day or the next. We lived in the cubicle for a whole week, while mom made arrangements to move out of the compound. She and her brother discussed this at length and he kept apologizing for not being able to accommodate us for a longer period.

The next place I found myself was in a town where Aunty Ata lives. She is mom's older sister as you already know. The first time I saw her, I was terrified by her looks. I'm not sure what her body size was when you last saw her. But she was a plump and very light-complexioned woman who wore a stony face all the time. Her face made me think about what her heart might also look like. She spoke a little and rarely smiled. I think she despises you and your family a lot; all her actions and words clearly spelt it out.

"Take the children back to your husband's people and come back to live your life, I will not train other people's children."

That was her constant reminder to mom, who didn't budge to any of her threats. Disregarding Aunty Ata had infuriated her so that she stirred up people against mom, as those who call her for menial jobs and harvesting of crops at the farms, gradually stopped doing so. Living with Aunty Ata was worse than living in Uncle Ben's and it left me wondering why an older sister would be so cruel to her younger sister with children. Isn't blood thicker than wine…sorry, water again? The most confusing part of the whole situation is that our family once lived in a bungalow of four rooms and a big palour. Mom had people who helped her with her catering business live with us and we can not go back to that house and live there, why? We merely went about like fugitives fleeing their homes. Why can't we go back there and stop bothering mom's family like a plague? I'm sure that I must have frustrated mom as a toddler with my annoying questions about our former house. I don't remember what her reaction was though. I wondered as a child, what we did so wrong that everybody didn't want us around, not even mom's family. Now, as an adult I have come to realise that marriage isn't only between lovers but between two families which must give their blessings. Why didn't you get them before your union?

As the strong and wise woman that she was and is, nom was able to rent a room from her savings. It was one of those moments that I had seen her smile so brightly because a burden out of several had been lifted. The church we attended was exceptionally generous with the provisions of a mattress, curtains, and a table while mom did a good job putting the room in order. The room gets extremely cold at night, so mom made us wear multiple clothes in the evening to avoid catching a cold. We would eat a particular food all through the week because that was what your wife could afford. I did cry and rejected the food a lot of times which made her very sad and angry. Sometimes, like a mad woman, she would scream at me "did your father's people send in your feeding allowance this month and I don't know about it? Ehn! Tell me," she would ask.

"Why don't you want to understand that in our condition, it's not a question of 'do you like your food and are you satisfied?' the question is rather if you have eaten!" she would set me straight. She would later break down in tears saying, "my dear, I am trying, ok, I am trying."

While living with mom and little Williams, I don't think I remembered having other siblings. Mom didn't talk about them either, so it just looked like it had always been you, mom, me, and little Williams all along. Sadly, mom came back home one day with her eyes red and swollen, she obviously looked like someone who had been crying for decades. I was confused because she would only cry openly in our presence whenever I cry and say "If dad was here, I won't be eating this kind of food." I promise you that wasn't what happened.

"My girls!" she sobbed while sitting on the floor. Who are her girls? Aren't I the only girl? I wanted to know so badly that I forgot to console her but asked questions instead.

"Who are your girls, mom?"

"Your sisters, Tope and Lilian." She said with tears trickling down her lean soft cheeks which have been ravaged by intense hardship and restlessness. Yet, even when she cried, she was still beautiful to behold. It was at that moment that it dawned on me that I had sisters! How could I have forgotten them in so short a time? I have no idea why I couldn't remember them but remembered you every day. I'm not sure I believed mom immediately that I had two sisters stuck somewhere with a family that was maltreating them, but I'm sure that I wanted to see them to verify her claims.

"I have to go and bring them back" she suddenly declared rising from the floor.

"Mom, are we going with you?" I asked feeling excited at the thought of travelling again. I was already used to moving from one place to another within a short time. I was always looking forward to when we'd move to another place forgetting that I was yet to start schooling as a result.

"No," she answered firmly, "you will stay at home and look after your brother while I'm gone."

There is no way in the world this woman would plan her escape using some sisters to fool me. I was not going to live in this world with both parents gone. Never! So, I probed her intensely.

"Mom, are you tired of me and Willie?" I whimpered.

"No!" her reply was sharp and signalled disappointment and sorrow.

"Mom, are you also travelling just like dad did?"

"No. Angela, listen to me…" she said as she tried to hold me but I ran away and stood by the door.

"You are lying so that you can go away because you are always sad. That is how dad left without telling you where he went to." I continued throwing tantrums. Mom walked outside and took me by the hand.

"No, I will never do that to you and your brother. Come, let's go inside."

She brought out a family portrait and showed me, my so-called sisters. The striking resemblance was the deal breaker for me! Now I could see why the old lady back in Akeh remarked that mom would have a difficult time looking at my face because, my siblings and me all look like you, I am the exact spitting image of you. Looking at the little me on your laps in that portrait confirms it. Mom explained that they were being mistreated by the family she had sent them to live with while we were still in Akeh. Someone whom she met while on a menial job hunt that evening had narrated how gaunt her daughters looked. Worse still, they were out of school and were 'sales girls' at the cement store of the lady of the house, mom's friend. I don't blame the family for not putting my sisters in school. Mom couldn't put Willie and me in school either as well. Although, she strived to feed us better though.

I sincerely wished for her to take us along with her. But like a mind reader, she again explained why she couldn't and that broke my heart. I had no definite feeling at that moment. They were all mixed up and it felt like I was going to die from feeling very feverish, trembling hands, a weak heart skidding rapidly, and a severe sudden migraine. I prayed to God silently to bring back the girls and mom safely if she ever travelled.

Dad, do you know how frightened I was when your wife left little Willie with me and went looking for my sisters? I was only 9 years old while Willie was 4. She entrusted us in the care of her landlady and took off very early on Saturday with the promise to return latest in the evening. Willie and I ate and played on the sandy street as we look out for mom's appearance with the girls. Willie cried a lot in the afternoon and the landlady had to give him a cold bath to calm him down. We sat under the almond tree in front of the house and waited for mom, but she didn't show up. I was hopeful until 9 pm before I lost it completely. Mom had left us! She has made me an accidental parent at just 9 and it was frightening. Willie wouldn't sleep except he puts his head on mom's chest, so I had to offer him my little chest for him to sleep. There was no electricity so I lit the lamp and left it in the centre of the room. The room was exceptionally dark, cold, and dreary that night. I was afraid to shut my eyes because I feared I may disappear with my dream and leave my brother behind. I cried so much that I could feel my spirit leaving my body.

I woke up with chest pain and more disappointment. Mom hadn't come back and I feared the worst had occurred. I won't bore you with the rest of our agonies. But unlike you, happily, mom came back from her travel after three days. So I reckon your destination is farther than imagined in my little head.

The struggle for survival became harder since mom had two extra mouths to feed. It was quite hard to eat what we liked. As a matter of fact, we couldn't even eat what we don't like to our fill. We rarely had a three-square meal except for Willie. Out of the little we had, mom would still generously give out to those who had nothing. Well, dad, I must confess that I hated that and I would complain bitterly every time a particular woman came begging. Though I never told anyone. Thinking back now, I knock myself very hard for having such selfish thoughts. The truth was, dad, I wasn't completely happy that my sisters returned because they were eating way too much that I felt they eat part of my ration with theirs. Also, the attention I received from mom seemed to have reduced. The only thing I was grateful for back then was having a warm family and big sisters who looked out for me. Though we had our internal fights, especially Tope and Lillian, mom always ensured they reconciled before bedtime.

Dad, let me skip to the good part because you may be sad to know that all that I have to tell you are sad memories. Well, it is not deliberate to make you feel pain. It is so just necessary to give you a peek at a few of the many things that have shaped our lives. If you're wondering if we are now living fine, then let your spirit peacefully rest because we are. Though not exactly how we would have lived if you hadn't left. Just like other kids, we dared to dream, especially me. I dreamed big but there was little or nothing to fund these dreams, hence we were forced to archive them and took the ones hard work, perseverance, and fate threw at us. Do you still remember how passionate Tope was about becoming a lawyer? She's now a seamstress. Lillian didn't become a nurse either because mom couldn't afford the tuition, but she could for a Food Technology course. However, thanks to them, mom got to wear gorgeous native clothes and eat sumptuous meals she couldn't while she toiled to raise us. I didn't become an architect like you though. This isn't due to a lack of funds. I didn't have the skill to become one no matter how hard I tried. I am a teacher instead and it brings me loads of gratification but little money to see young people I've imparted knowledge. We may have turned out differently from what you expected, but we are all ensuring that you'd look down beneath you and see Willie fly an aeroplane through the sky someday. It's all he ever wants to do.

Dear dad, let me congratulate you albeit belatedly on the marriage of your two daughters to the men of their dreams. Let me also quickly add that you are now a grandfather to three handsome boys! How about me, you may want to ask. Dad, I haven't been lucky in love. But I'm seeing someone at the moment who reminds me of you. Hopefully, he's the one.

I'm going to bring my letter to a close now, knowing that signing off this way would bring you a more restful soul. I'm glad to tell you that we've made progress compared to how we used to live without you. Though, it may seem like no progress is made because it hasn't been rapid and smooth. Looking back, I know more than anyone that we've made progress. You should be proud of us, dad. Lest I forget, mom is basking in the euphoria of visiting every one of us. She still helps to solve problems. She's always full of smiles and talks about when she'll finally be reunited with you. Don't get too excited yet because you'd have to wait a long time to see her again.

Hey dad, my best friend and the painful memory I never would let go, please, go back to rest in peace until we meet to part no more.

Love,

Angie

www.ingramcontent.com/pod-product-compliance
Lightning Source LLC
La Vergne TN
LVHW052116160826
845678LV00015B/3585

* 9 7 9 8 3 6 7 9 2 3 7 3 5 *